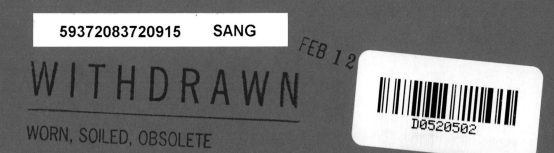

Kate & Pippin

An Unlikely
Love Story

Martin Springett

Photographs by Isobel Springett

Henry Holt and Company · New York

The fawn lay still and quiet. She was alone and afraid as she waited for her mother to come back.

Every little deer needs its mother to protect it from the many dangers of the forest.

But her mother did not return, and three long days passed.

Finally, as the hungry fawn cried, friendly hands lifted her up.

They gently carried her away from the field where she had been hiding and brought her to a nearby house.

Kate, a Great Dane, was asleep on her comfy round bed when she felt a small, warm presence.

She was surprised to see a fawn lying beside her!

Kate gave the young deer a nuzzle and a lick.

The fawn was certain she had found a
new mother. She snuggled in close to Kate
and gave a soft cry.

Kate had never had puppies of her own.
But she was a gentle dog, and being a mom
to the little deer came naturally.

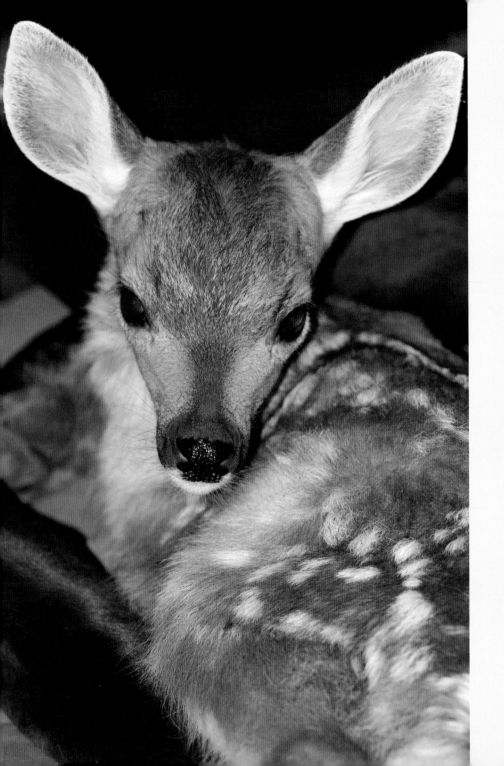

Watching them together,
Kate's owner, Isobel, realized
the fawn might be staying
with them for a while and
would need a name.

Isobel decided on Pippin—
the sound of the name suited
the tiny deer perfectly.

Even though she was hungry, Pippin didn't know what to make of the baby bottle that Isobel offered her.

At first she bit the bottle, and she was disappointed when she couldn't get at the sheep's milk inside.

Gradually she calmed down and began to suck. After two days of practice, Pippin was feeding contentedly.

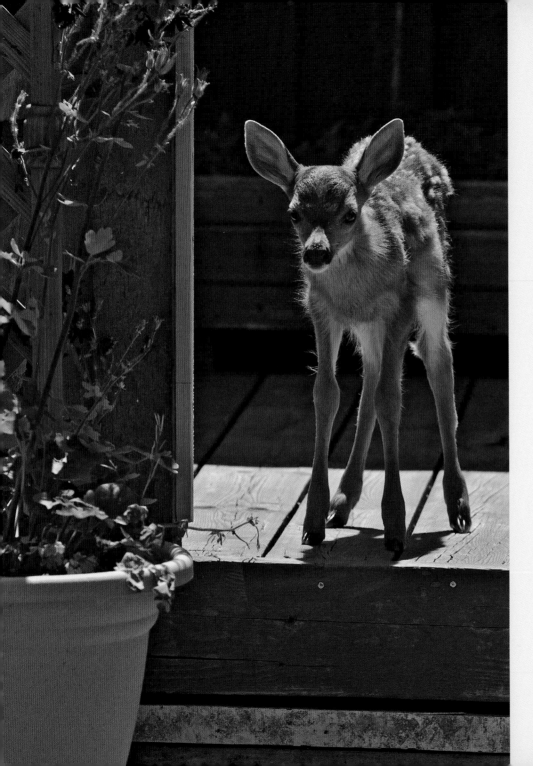

As Pippin grew, her bond with Kate also grew. She followed the big black dog everywhere, just as a puppy would follow its mother.

After a week indoors, gaining strength and confidence, Pippin took her first steps outside. She made her way to the short set of stairs that led to the garden.

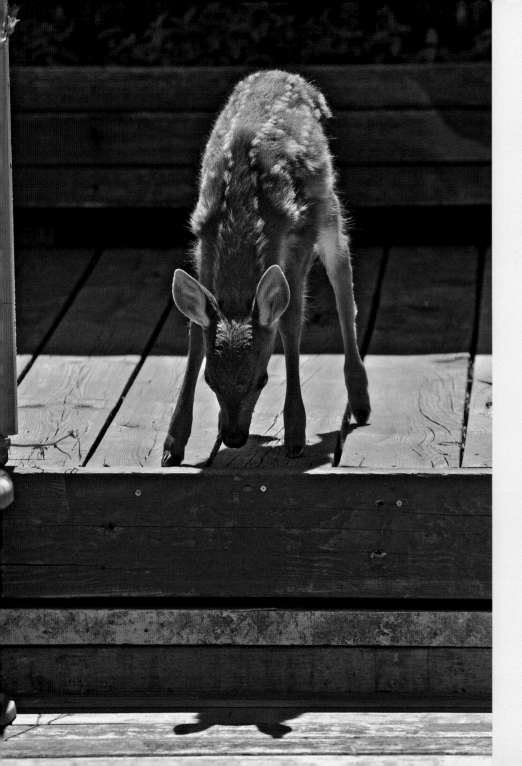

The stairs were a
challenge for the fawn,
but she eventually
stepped down onto
the grass.

Outside, Kate and Pippin began to play!
They rolled around on the lawn and chased
each other, running and leaping everywhere.
Then they returned to the house to sleep.

One evening, though, the fawn did not return to the house. Isobel called to her, and Kate waited patiently for her to come home, but she had disappeared into the forest.

Kate and Isobel worried they might never see Pippin again.

They were both up early the next morning,
waiting.

Finally, at the edge of the trees, the long grass
rustled and Pippin came into view! She trotted
up to Kate and made a little greeting sound
before asking to be fed.

From then on, Pippin slept in the forest each night but came back almost every morning. She loved to run around the farm, playing with her mom and enjoying snacks from Isobel, like bananas and bread.

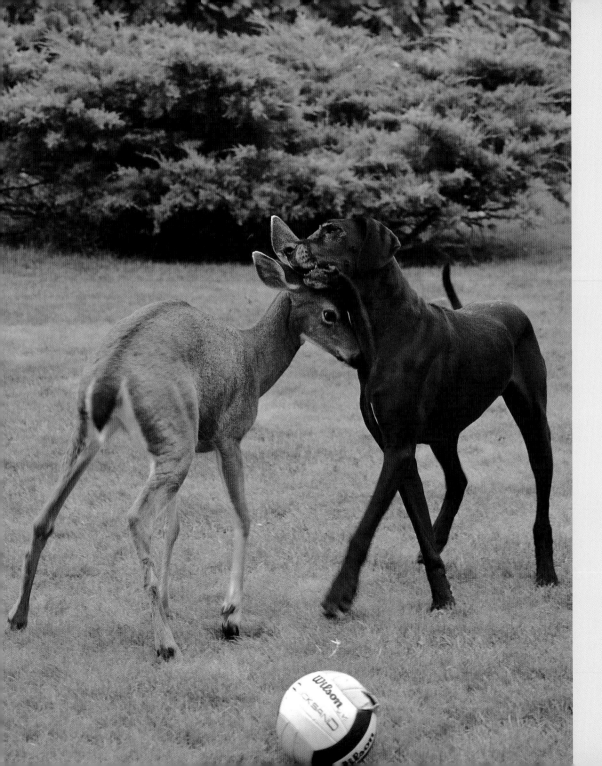

Pippin grew up quickly, but she was still Kate's little pup.

She made other animal friends, too, including Henry the cat, who had lived with Kate for many years.

Henry did not want a bath every time she visited, but he let Pippin clean him with her long pink tongue.

Pippin gradually became an independent deer. She no longer needed to be bottle-fed, and she foraged on plants and grasses in the forest.

But even when she was fully grown, Pippin always came back to the farm to play with Kate.

Sometimes, Pippin still invites herself into the house for a visit. Pippin is a wild animal and the forest is her home, but she and Kate remain the best of friends.

This book is for our mother, Joan Springett.

Henry Holt and Company, LLC
Publishers since 1866
175 Fifth Avenue
New York, New York 10010
mackids.com

Henry Holt® is a registered trademark of Henry Holt and Company, LLC.
Text copyright © 2012 by Martin Springett
Photographs copyright © 2012 by Isobel Springett
All rights reserved.
Simultaneously published in Canada by Penguin Group (Canada), a division
of Pearson Canada Inc.

Library of Congress Cataloging-in-Publication Data
Springett, Martin.
Kate and Pippin / Martin Springett ; photos by Isobel Springett. — 1st ed.
p.   cm.
ISBN 978-0-8050-9487-9 (hc)
1. Fawns—Juvenile fiction. 2. Great Dane—Juvenile fiction. [1. Deer—Fiction.
2. Great Dane—Fiction. 3. Dogs—Fiction. 4. Animals—Infancy—Fiction.
5. Parental behavior in animals—Fiction.] I. Springett, Isobel, ill. II. Title.
PZ10.3.S6833Kat 2012   [E]—dc23   2011033499

First American Edition—2012 / Designed by Elynn Cohen
Printed in the United States of America by Worzalla, Stevens Point, Wisconsin

10 9 8 7 6 5 4 3 2 1